made of magic.

P. Marin

It is easy to feel small and
underwhelming, to forget
the magic you are made of.

That is why we are watering
our magic, to remind us we are
worth believing in. We are
worth caring for and loving.
We are worth all the bubble
baths. Hold on to your rubber
duck or your warty toad.

You are worth all the love.

Watering magic is a lot like hatching

Butterflies...

We discover our magic in our own time. Did you know a caterpillar must dissolve within its cocoon before it emerges as a butterfly? Things happen in stages. Sometimes a meltdown is part of the process. There is a butterfly in each of us. Do not give up before you get your wings.

You do not have to pull a rabbit from the hat.

Just water your magic every day. Its roots will grow
deep and strong.

It starts with believing. Believing you can do those things you thought you could not. Knowing you are made for something more.

We are all *Unicorns*
in our own ways.

Even when you are standing on your own two feet or soaking in your clawfoot bathtub, you are not alone. There is someone behind the scenes orchestrating this magical life. So in addition to reaching for your rubber duck and your bubble bath, reach for the stars. Someone is working hard to bring them within reach.

When you finally say to yourself, "I am made of magic," the skies may not open and the waters may not part. But the ripple that stirs within will move your feet wildly in the direction of your dreams.

Owning your magic takes courage.
I see how brave you are.

Life does not always go as planned. Be gentle with yourself. Be gentle with the ones sitting next to you. We are all doing the best we can.

Self-care is not a luxury. It is a prerequisite for compassion. It is a necessary and crucial part of owning your magic.
Be good to you.

Arm's length may feel safer, but let us not forget what happens when you open your heart and someone squeezes in. There is magic in those moments too.

Look me in the eye...

Snails are made of magic. You can tell—not because they paint with the verve of da Vinci or because their Italian love songs make you weak in the knees—but because of how they look at you. Slowly. With care. Like you are the only one who matters.

Look me in
the eye while
I tell you
I see the
magic you
are made of.

There is a seed of magic in each of us.
It is never too late to begin watering.

The real question is not what you are
made of, but how to fit all that magic into
one tiny tub.

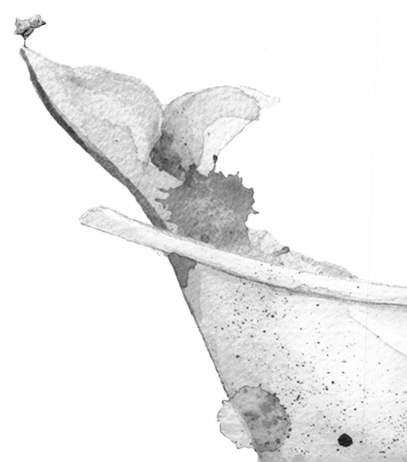

We are worth believing in.
Every last one of us.

No exceptions.

Author's Note:

I am a firm believer that each of us has something unique to share with this world. We are made of magic and when we water that magic, our confidence grows. Our worth and value bloom. It is from this place of self-love and compassion that we are able to do the important work of caring for ourselves and the world around us.

Hocus-pocus, alakazam!
Help me to remember who I am.
Presto.

You are Magic.
xo
P. Marin

To Marco and to Marin.
I see your magic.
PM

The Goal is Magic

Prints Marin, Ink, Huntington Beach, CA

P. Marin

The Goal is Magic

ISBN-10: 0-9986119-6-4   ISBN-13: 978-0-9986119-6-9

PRINTS MARIN, INK
Find what you love and do it often.
pmarin.com

Made in the USA
Columbia, SC
19 November 2024

46576942R00020